# Medical Spanish In Simple Terms

## Simply, The Key Terms to Learn

José Luis Leyva

Idea Editorial – www.ideaeditorial.com

ISBN: 1507617534
ISBN-13: 978-1507617533

# PREFACE

This book is intended to assist healthcare professionals to learn just the key medical terms in Spanish. Rather than a thick dictionary, filled with explanations and multiple entries, *Medical Spanish In Simple Terms* will be a handy book that can be used to learn the key medical terminology in Spanish. Learn a few terms each day, and soon you will be acquainted with the most common medical terminology in English and Spanish.

ENGLISH-SPANISH
INGLÉS-ESPAÑOL

# A

**abdomen,** abdomen

**abdominal,** abdominal

**abnormal,** anormal

**abortion,** aborto

**abrasion,** abrasión/raspadura

**abscess,** absceso

**abstinence,** abstinencia

**abuse,** abuso

**accident,** accidente

**acetaminophen,** acetaminofén

**ache,** dolor

**acid,** ácido

**acne,** acné

**active,** activo

**acute,** agudo

**addict,** adicto

**addiction,** adicción

**admit (into hospital),** ingresar

**adolescence,** adolescencia

**adopt (to),** adoptar

**adult,** adulto

**adrenaline,** adrenalina

**advise (to),** aconsejar

**afterbirth,** placenta

**agitation,** agitación

**ailment,** enfermedad

**air,** aire

**alcoholism,** alcoholismo

**alive,** vivo

**allergic,** alérgico

**allergy,** alergia

**ambulance,** ambulancia

**amenorrhea,** amenorrea

**amino acid,** aminoácido

**ammonia,** amoníaco

**amnesia,** amnesia

**amniocentesis,** amniocentesis

**amniotic sac,** bolsa amniótica

**amphetamines,** anfetaminas

**amputate (to),** amputar

**analgesic,** analgésico

**analysis,** análisis

**anaphylactic,** shock anafiláctico

**anatomy,** anatomía

**anemia,** anemia

**anemic,** anémico

**anesthesia,** anestesia

**anesthesiologist,** anestesiólogo

**aneurysm/aneurism,** aneurisma

**anger,** enojo

**angiogram,** angiograma

**angioplasty,** angioplastia

**anorexia,** anorexia

**antacid,** antiácido

**anthrax,** ántrax

**antibiotic,** antibiótico

**antibodies,** anticuerpos

**anticoagulant,** anticoagulante

**antidepressant,** antidepresivo

**antidote,** antídoto

**antihistamine,** antihistamínico

**anus,** ano

**anxiety,** ansiedad

**aorta,** aorta

**apathy,** apatía

**apnea,** apnea

**appendectomy,** apendectomía

**appendicitis,** apendicitis

**appetite,** apetito

**applicator,** aplicador

**appointment,** cita

**arm,** brazo

**arm pit,** axila

**arrhythmia,** arritmia

**artery,** arteria

**arthritis,** artritis

**asphyxia,** asfixia

**asthma,** asma

**asthmatic,** asmático

**astigmatism,** astigmatismo

**athlete's foot,** pie de atleta

**atrophy,** atrofia

**autism,** autismo

**autopsy,** autopsia

**awake,** despierto

**awaken (to),** despertar

# B

**baby,** bebé

**back,** espalda

**backbone,** columna vertebral

**bacteria,** bacteria

**bad,** malo(a)

**balance,** equilibrio

**bald,** calvo

**baldness,** calvicie

**bandage,** vendaje

**bandaid,** curita

**barbiturates,** barbitúricos

**barium,** bario

**basin,** palangana

**bath,** baño

**bathe (to),** bañarse

**bed,** cama

**bedpan,** orinal

**bedridden (patient),** encamado

**bed-wetting,** enuresis

**behavior,** conducta

**belch,** eructo

**belly,** vientre

**bellybutton,** ombligo

**benign,** benigno

**bib,** babero

**biceps,** bíceps

**bicuspid,** bicúspide

**bile,** bilis

**bilirubin,** bilirrubina

**biological,** biológico

**biopsy,** biopsia

**birth,** nacimiento/parto

**birthmark,** lunar

**bite,** mordedura

**bite (insect),** picadura

**bitter,** amargo

**blackheads,** espinillas

**bladder,** vejiga

**bleed,** sangrar

**blind,** ciego

**blindness,** ceguera

**blink,** parpadear

**blister,** ampolla

**blockage,** obstrucción

**blood,** sangre

**body,** cuerpo

**bone,** hueso

**booster shot,** vacuna de refuerzo

**bottle,** botella

**botulism,** botulismo

**bowel,** intestino

**brace,** aparato ortopédico

**braces (dental),** frenos dentales

**brain,** cerebro

**break,** quebrar

**breast/chest,** pecho/seno

**breastbone,** esternón

**breath,** aliento

**breathe,** respirar

**broken,** roto

**bronchitis,** bronquitis

**bruise,** moretón

**bruised,** amoratado

**bulimia,** bulimia

**bulimic,** bulímico

**bump,** protuberancia

**bunion,** juanete

**burn,** quemadura

**burp,** eructar

**bursitis,** bursitis

**buttock,** glúteo

**buzzing,** zumbido

# C

**calcified,** calcificado

**calcium,** calcio

**calf (of leg),** pantorilla

**callus,** callo

**calorie,** caloría

**cancer,** cáncer

**cancerous,** canceroso

**cane,** bastón

**capillary,** capilar

**capsule,** cápsula

**carbohydrate,** carbohidrato

**carcinogenic,** carcinogénico

**carcinoma,** carcinoma

**cardiac,** cardíaco

**cardiologist,** cardiólogo

**cardiology,** cardiología

**care,** cuidado

**cartilage,** cartílago

**cast,** yeso

**castration,** castración

**cataract,** catarata

**catatonic,** catatónico

**catheter,** catéter

**catheterization,** cateterismo

**catheterize,** cateterizar

**cause,** causa

**cauterize,** cauterizar

**cervix,** cuello del útero

**chafe,** rozar

**checkup,** examen

**cheek,** mejilla

**chemical,** químico

**chemotherapy,** quimioterapia

**chest,** pecho

**chew,** masticar

**chicken pox,** varicela

**childbirth,** parto

**childhood,** infancia

**chills,** escalofríos

**chin,** barbilla

**chiropractor,** quiropráctico

**chlamydia,** clamidia

**choke,** ahogarse

**cholera,** cólera

**cholesterol,** colesterol

**chronic,** crónico

**cigarette,** cigarrillo

**circulation,** circulación

**circumcision,** circuncisión

**cirrhosis,** cirrosis

**claustrophobia,** claustrofobia

**cleft palate,** paladar hendido

**clinic,** clínica

**clitoris,** clítoris

**clot,** coágulo

**cocaine,** cocaína

**coccyx,** cóccix

**codeine,** codeína

**cold,** frío/a

**cold (illness),** resfriado común

**cold sores,** herpes labial

**colic,** cólico

**colitis,** colitis

**collagen,** colágeno

**collarbone,** clavícula

**colon,** colon

**colonoscopy,** colonoscopía

**color-blindness,** daltonismo

**colostomy,** colostomia

**coma,** coma

**comatose,** comatoso

**comfortable,** cómodo

**complaint,** queja

**complexion,** tez

**complication,** complicación

**compress,** compresa

**conceive,** concebir

**concussion,** conmoción cerebral

**condom,** condón

**confused,** confundido

**confusion,** confusión

**congenital,** congénito

**congested (to be),** estar congestionado

**congestion,** congestión

**conjunctiva,** conjuntiva

**conjunctivitis,** conjuntivitis

**conscious,** consciente

**consciousness,** conocimiento

**consent,** consentir

**constipation,** estreñimiento

**contagious,** contagioso

**contaminated,** contaminado

**contraception,** anticoncepción

**contractions,** contracciones

**contusion,** contusión

**convalescent,** convaleciente

**convulsion,** convulsión

**corn (callus),** callo

**coronary,** coronario

**cortisone,** cortisona

**cough,** tos

**cough,** toser

**CPR,** reanimación cardiopulmonar

**crabs,** ladillas

**cramp,** calambre

**cramps (menstrual),** cólicos menstruales

**cranium,** cráneo

**craving,** antojo

**crawl,** gatear

**crib,** cuna

**cripple,** lisiar

**crippled,** lisiado

**critical,** crítico

**Crohn's disease,** enfermedad de Crohn

**cross-eyed,** bizco

**croup,** crup

**crutches,** muletas

**cry,** llorar

**CT scan,** tomografía por computadora

**culture,** cultivo

**cure,** curar

**cut,** cortar

**cuticle,** cutícula

**cyst,** quiste

**cystic fibrosis,** fibrosis quística

# D

**daily,** diariamente

**dandruff,** caspa

**danger,** peligro

**daze,** aturdimiento

**dead,** muerto

**deaf,** sordo

**deaf-mute,** sordomudo

**deafness,** sordera

**death,** muerte

**deceased,** difunto

**decongestant,** descongestionante

**defecate,** defecar

**defibrillation,** desfibrilación

**defibrillator,** desfibrilador

**deficiency,** deficiencia

**deformed,** deformado

**deformity,** deformidad

**dehydration,** deshidratación

**delirious,** delirante

**delirium,** delirio

**delivery (of a baby),** parto

**deltoids,** deltoides

**dementia,** demencia

**dental,** dental

**dentist,** dentista

**denture,** dentadura postiza

**depigmentation,** despigmentación

**depression,** depresión

**dermatitis,** dermatitis

**dermatologist,** dermatólogo

**deterioration,** deterioro

**detoxification,** desintoxicación

**develop,** desarrollar

**diabetes,** diabetes

**diagnose,** diagnosticar

**diagnosis,** diagnóstico

**dialysis,** diálisis

**diaper,** pañal

**diaphragm,** diafragma

**diarrhea,** diarrea

**die,** morir

**diet,** dieta

**dietitian,** dietista

**digest,** digerir

**digestion,** digestión

**dilated,** dilatado

**dilation,** dilatación

**dilute,** diluir

**diphtheria,** difteria

**disability,** discapacidad

**discharge,** secreción

**discharge from hospital,** dar de alta

**discontinue,** suspender

**disease,** enfermedad

**disinfect,** desinfectar

**disinfectant,** desinfectante

**disk (slipped),** disco desplazado

**dislocation,** dislocación

**disorder,** trastorno

**disorientation,** desorientación

**distend,** distender

**distressed,** angustiado

**diuretic,** diurético

**dizziness,** mareos

**dizzy,** mareado

**doctor,** médico

**doctor's office,** consultorio

**donor,** donante

**dosage,** dosis

**double vision,** vista doble

**drain,** supurar

**draw blood,** sacar sangre

**dropper,** gotero

**drops,** gotas

**drowning,** ahogamiento

**drowsy,** somnoliento

**drug addiction,** adicción a las drogas

**drugs (usually illicit),** drogas

**drugs (legal),** medicinas

**drunk,** borracho

**dryness,** sequedad

**due date,** fecha aproximada de parto

**dull (pain),** sordo (dolor)

**duodenum,** duodeno

**dust,** polvo

**dwarfism,** enanismo

**dysentery,** disentería

**dyslexia,** dislexia

**dystrophy,** distrofia

# E

**ear (inner),** oído

**ear (middle),** oído medio

**ear (outer),** oreja

**earache,** dolor de oído

**eardrum,** tímpano

**earlobe,** lóbulo

**earplugs,** tapones para los oídos

**eczema,** eccema

**edema,** edema

**egg,** huevo/óvulo

**ejaculate,** eyacular

**EKG,** electrocardiograma

**elbow,** codo

**elderly,** anciano

**electrocardiogram,** electrocardiograma

**electrocution,** electrocución

**elixir,** elixir

**emaciated,** escuálido

**embolism,** embolia

**embryo,** embrión

**emergency,** emergencia

**pulmonary emphysema,** enfisema pulmonar

**encephalitis,** encefalitis

**endemic,** endémico

**endocrine,** endocrino

**endocrinologist,** endocrinólogo

**endorphin,** endorfina

**endoscopy,** endoscopía

**enema,** enema

**enlargement,** agrandamiento

**enzyme,** enzima

**epidemic,** epidémico/epidemia

**epidural,** epidural

**epiglottis,** epiglotis

**epilepsy,** epilepsia

**erection,** erección

**esophagus,** esófago

**estrogen,** estrógeno

**ether,** éter

**euphoria,** euforia

**Eustachian tube,** trompa de Eustaquio

**euthanasia,** eutanasia

**exam,** examen

**examine,** examinar

**excrement,** excremento

**exercise,** ejercicio

**exertion,** esfuerzo

**exfoliation,** exfoliación

**exhale,** exhalar

**exhaustion,** agotamiento

**expectorant,** expectorante

**expert,** experto

**explain,** explicar

**exposure,** exposición

**external,** externo

**extract,** extraer

**extraction,** extracción

**eye,** ojo

**eyebrow,** ceja

**eyelash,** pestaña

**eyelid,** párpado

**eyesight,** vista

# F

**face,** cara

**face down,** boca abajo

**face up,** boca arriba

**faint,** desmayarse

**fainting spells,** desmayos

**fall,** caída

**Fallopian tubes,** trompas de Falopio

**false teeth,** dientes postizos

**family planning,** planificación familiar

**fast,** ayunar

**fat (food),** grasa

**fat (person),** gordo

**fatal,** fatal/mortal

**fatigue,** fatiga

**fear,** miedo

**feces,** heces

**feed,** alimentar

**feel,** sentir

**feet,** pies

**femur,** fémur

**fertile,** fértil

**fertilization,** fertilización

**fetal monitor,** monitor fetal

**fetus,** feto

**fever,** fiebre

**fiber,** fibra

**fibrillation,** fibrilación

**filling (dental),** empaste

**finger,** dedo (de la mano)

**finger pad,** yema

**fire,** fuego/incendio

**first aid,** primeros auxilios

**fissure,** fisura

**fist,** puño

**flake,** escama

**flat foot,** pie plano

**flatulence,** flatulencia

**flexible,** flexible

**flu,** gripe

**fluoride,** fluoruro

**flush,** rubor

**foam,** espuma

**folic acid,** ácido fólico

**folk healer,** curandero

**follicle,** folículo

**follow-up,** examen de seguimiento

**food,** alimentos

**foot,** pie

**forceps,** fórceps

**forearm,** antebrazo

**forehead,** frente

**foreskin,** prepucio

**form,** formulario

**formula,** fórmula

**fracture,** fractura

**freckle,** peca

**freeze,** congelar

**frequency,** frecuencia

**fright,** susto

**function,** función

**fungus,** hongo

# G

**gag,** provocar náuseas

**gain weight,** subir de peso

**gall bladder,** vesícula biliar

**gallstones,** cálculos biliares

**gangrene,** gangrena

**gargle,** hacer gárgaras

**gas,** gas

**gash,** tajo

**gastric ulcer,** úlcera gástrica

**gastritis,** gastritis

**gastroenterologist,** gastroenterólogo

**gastrointestinal (GI),** gastrointestinal

**gauze,** gasa

**gel,** gel

**gender,** sexo

**genes,** genes

**genetic,** genético

**genitals,** genitales

**geriatric,** geriátrico

**germ,** germen

**German measles,** rubéola

**gestation,** gestación

**gigantism,** gigantismo

**giardia,** giardia

**gingivitis,** gingivitis

**gland,** glándula

**glasses,** gafas

**glaucoma,** glaucoma

**glove,** guante

**glucose,** glucosa

**gluten,** gluten

**goiter,** bocio

**gonorrhea,** gonorrea

**goose bumps,** piel de gallina

**gout,** gota

**gown,** bata

**graft,** injerto

**gram,** gramo

**grief,** pesar

**grieve,** afligirse

**grind,** moler

**groin,** ingle

**growth,** crecimiento

**guilt,** culpa

**gums,** encías

**gun,** pistola

**gurney,** camilla

**gut,** intestino/tripas

**gynecologist,** ginecólogo

**gynecology,** ginecología

# H

**habit,** hábito

**hair,** pelo

**hair (body),** vello

**halitosis,** mal aliento

**hallucination,** alucinación

**hammer,** martillo de reflejos

**hamstring,** músculo posterior del muslo

**hand,** mano

**hangnail,** padrastro

**hangover,** resaca

**hardening,** endurecimiento

**harm,** dañar

**harmful,** dañino

**harmless,** inofensivo

**head,** cabeza

**headache,** dolor de cabeza

**heal,** curarse

**health,** salud

**health care,** atención a la salud

**healthy,** sano

**hear,** oír

**hearing,** audición

**heart,** corazón

**heart attack,** ataque cardíaco

**heartbeat,** latido del corazón

**heartburn,** acidez estomacal

**heat-stroke,** insolación

**heating pad,** cojín eléctrico

**heel,** talón

**height,** altura

**helicopter,** helicóptero

**hematoma,** hematoma

**hemoglobin,** hemoglobina

**hemophilia,** hemofilia

**hemorrhage,** hemorragia

**hepatitis,** hepatitis

**herb,** hierba

**herbalist,** yerbero

**hereditary,** hereditario

**heredity,** herencia

**hermaphrodite,** hermafrodita

**hernia,** hernia

**heroin,** heroína

**herpes,** herpes

**heterosexual,** heterosexual

**hiccups,** hipo

**high blood pressure,** presión alta

**hip,** cadera

**hives,** ronchas

**hoarse,** ronco

**hoarseness,** ronquera

**homeopathy,** homeopatía

**homosexual,** homosexual

**hookworm,** anquilostomosis

**hormonal,** hormonal

**hormone,** hormona

**hospital,** hospital

**hospitalize,** internar

**hot flashes,** sofocos

**hunchback,** jorobado

**hurt,** doler

**hydrate,** hidratar

**hydrogen peroxide,** peróxido de hidrógeno

**hygiene,** higiene

**hymen,** himen

**hyperactive,** hiperactivo

**hyperglycemia,** hiperglucemia

**hypersensitivity,** hipersensibilidad

**hypertension,** presión alta

**hyperthermia,** hipertermia

**hyperthyroidism,** hipertiroidismo

**hyperventilation,** hiperventilación

**hypochondria,** hipocondria

**hypoglycemia,** hipoglucemia

**hypothalamus,** hipotálamo

**hypothermia,** hipotermia

**hypothyroidism,** hipotiroidismo

**hypoxia,** hipoxia

**hysterectomy,** histerectomía

**hysteria,** histeria

# I

**ibuprofen,** ibuprofeno

**ill,** enfermo

**illness,** enfermedad

**immature,** inmaduro

**immobile,** inmóvil

**immobilization,** inmovilización

**immune,** inmune

**immunize,** inmunizar

**impacted tooth,** diente impactado

**impaired,** dañado

**impairment,** incapacidad

**implant,** implantar

**impotence,** impotencia

**impregnation,** fecundación

**incest,** incesto

**incision,** incisión

**incontinence,** incontinencia

**incubator,** incubadora

**incurable,** incurable

**indigestion,** indigestión

**induce,** inducir

**infant,** bebé

**infect,** infectar

**infection,** infección

**infertile,** estéril

**infertility,** infertilidad

**inflammation,** inflamación

**influenza,** gripe

**ingest,** ingerir

**inhale,** inhalar

**inhaler,** inhalador

**inject,** inyectar

**injury,** lesión

**inoculate,** inocular

**inoculation,** inoculación

**insane,** loco

**insanity,** locura

**insemination,** inseminación

**insomnia,** insomnio

**instrument,** instrumento

**insulin,** insulina

**insurance,** seguro

**intensive care,** terapia intensiva

**intercourse,** relaciones sexuales

**internal,** interno

**internist,** internista

**intestine,** intestino

**intoxication,** intoxicación

**intravenous fluids,** líquidos intravenosos

**intubation,** intubación

**iodine,** yodo

**iron,** hierro

**irregular heartbeat,** latidos cardíacos irregulares

**irrigate,** irrigar

**irritation,** irritación

**itch,** comezón

# J

**jaundice,** ictericia/piel amarilla

**jaw,** mandíbula

**jelly,** jalea

**jock itch,** tiña crural

**joint,** articulación

**jugular,** yugular

**juice,** jugo

# K

**kidney,** riñón

**kidney failure,** insuficiencia renal

**kidney stones,** cálculos renales

**knee,** rodilla

**kneecap,** rótula

**knife,** cuchillo

**knot,** nudo

**knuckle,** nudillo

# L

**labor,** trabajo de parto

**labor pains,** dolores de parto

**laboratory,** laboratorio

**labyrinthitis,** laberintitis

**laceration,** laceración

**lactation,** lactancia

**lactose,** lactosa

**lame extremity,** extremidad lisiada

**language,** lenguaje

**laparoscopy,** laparoscopía

**large intestine,** intestino grueso

**laryngitis,** laringitis

**larynx,** laringe

**laser treatment,** tratamiento con láser

**latex,** látex

**laughing gas,** gas hilarante (óxido nitroso)

**laxative,** laxante

**lead,** plomo

**leech,** sanguijuela

**left-handed,** zurdo

**leg,** pierna

**leprosy,** lepra

**lesbian,** lesbiana

**lesion,** lesión

**lethargy,** letargo

**leukemia,** leucemia

**libido,** deseo sexual

**lice,** piojos

**life,** vida

**lifestyle,** estilo de vida

**ligament,** ligamento

**light-headedness,** vahído

**limb,** extremidad

**liniment,** linimento

**liposuction,** liposucción

**lips,** labios

**liquid,** líquido

**lisp,** ceceo

**listen,** escuchar

**live,** vivir

**liver,** hígado

**lobe,** lóbulo

**lobotomy,** lobotomía

**lockjaw,** tétanos

**low blood pressure,** presión baja

**lozenges,** pastillas para la garganta

**lubricate,** lubricar

**lump,** bulto

**lumpectomy,** tumorectomía

**lungs,** pulmones

**lupus,** lupus

**lymph,** linfa

**lymph nodes,** ganglios linfáticos

**lymphoma,** linfoma

# M

**malabsorption,** malabsorción

**malaise,** malestar

**malaria,** paludismo

**male,** varón/masculino

**malformation,** malformación

**malignant,** maligno

**malnutrition,** desnutrición

**malpractice,** negligencia médica

**mammogram,** mamografía

**mania,** manía

**manic-depressive,** maníaco depresivo

**marijuana,** marihuana

**mask,** máscara

**mass,** masa

**massage/rub,** masajear

**mastectomy,** mastectomía

**maternal,** materno

**maturity,** madurez

**measles,** sarampión

**medical record,** expediente médico

**medication,** medicamento

**medicine,** medicina

**melanoma,** melanoma

**meningitis,** meningitis

**menopause,** menopausia

**menses,** menstruación

**menstrual cycle,** ciclo menstrual

**menstruation,** menstruación

**mental illness,** trastorno mental

**metabolism,** metabolismo

**metastasis,** metástasis

**methadone,** metadona

**methamphetamine,** metanfetamina

**microscope,** microscopio

**microsurgery,** microcirugía

**midwife,** partera

**migraine,** migraña

**mind,** mente

**miscarriage,** aborto natural

**mite,** ácaro

**mole,** lunar

**monitor,** monitor

**mononucleosis,** mononucleosis

**morgue,** morgue

**morphine,** morfina

**mortality,** mortalidad

**mouth,** boca

**mucous,** mucoso/mucosa

**mumps,** paperas

**muscle,** músculo

**mutation,** mutación

**mute,** mudo

**myopia,** miopía

# N

**nail,** uña

**naked,** desnudo

**nap,** siesta

**nape,** nuca

**narcolepsy,** narcolepsia

**narcotic,** narcótico

**natural,** natural

**nausea,** náuseas

**navel,** ombligo

**nearsightedness,** miopía

**neck,** cuello

**needle,** aguja

**nerve,** nervio

**nervous,** nervioso

**neuralgia,** neuralgia

**neurologist,** neurólogo

**neurology,** neurología

**neurosis,** neurosis

**neurotic,** neurótico

**nicotine,** nicotina

**nightmare,** pesadilla

**nipple,** pezón

**nitroglycerine,** nitroglicerina

**normal,** normal

**nose,** nariz

**nostril,** fosa nasal

**nourishment,** nutrición

**numbness,** adormecimiento

**nurse,** enfermera

**nutrient,** nutriente

**nutrition,** nutrición

**nutritionist,** nutricionista

# O

**obese,** obeso

**obesity,** obesidad

**obstetrician,** obstetra

**obstetrics,** obstetricia

**obstruction,** obstrucción

**occlusion,** oclusión

**odor,** olor

**office,** consultorio

**ointment,** ungüento

**oncologist,** oncólogo

**oncology,** oncología

**operate,** operar

**ophthalmologist, oftalmólogo,**

**optic,** óptico

**optometrist,** optometrista

**oral,** oral

**organ,** órgano

**orgasm,** orgasmo

**orthodontist,** ortodoncista

**orthopedics,** ortopedia

**orthopedist,** ortopedista

**osteoarthritis,** osteoartritis

**osteopath,** osteópata

**osteoporosis,** osteoporosis

**ovary,** ovario

**overdose,** sobredosis

**overweight,** sobrepeso

**ovulate,** ovular

**ovulation,** ovulación

**oxygen,** oxígeno

# P

**pacemaker,** marcapaso

**pacifier,** chupete

**pain,** dolor

**pain reliever,** calmante para el dolor

**painful,** doloroso

**palate,** paladar

**pale,** pálido

**paleness,** palidez

**palpitations,** palpitaciones

**pancreas,** páncreas

**Pap smear,** examen de Papanicolaou

**paralysis,** parálisis

**paralyzed,** paralítico

**paramedic,** paramédico

**paranoia,** paranoia

**paraplegic,** parapléjico

**parasite,** parásito

**patch,** parche

**paternal,** paterno

**pathologist,** patólogo

**patient,** paciente

**pediatric,** pediátrico

**pediatrician,** pediatra

**pediatrics,** pediatría

**pelvis,** pelvis

**penetrate,** penetrar

**penicillin,** penicilina

**penis,** pene

**perforation,** perforación

**perspire,** transpirar

**pertussis,** tos ferina

**pharmacist,** farmacéutico

**pharmacy,** farmacia

**pharynx,** faringe

**phlegm,** flema

**phobia,** fobia

**phosphorus,** fósforo

**photosensitivity,** fotosensibilidad

**physical therapy,** fisioterapia

**physician,** médico

**pill,** píldora

**pillow,** almohada

**pimples,** espinillas

**placenta,** placenta

**plague,** plaga

**plaque,** placa

**plasma,** plasma

**platelets,** plaquetas

**pneumonia,** pulmonía

**podiatrist,** podólogo

**poison,** veneno

**polio,** poliomielitis

**pollen,** polen

**polyp,** pólipo

**pore,** poro

**postmenopausal,** postmenopáusico

**post-op,** después de la operación

**postpartum,** posparto

**potassium,** potasio

**pound,** libra

**powder,** polvo

**predispose,** predisponer

**preeclampsia,** pre eclampsia

**pregnancy,** embarazo

**pregnant,** embarazada

**premature birth,** nacimiento prematuro

**premenopausal,** pre menopáusico

**prenatal care,** cuidado prenatal

**prescribe,** recetar

**prescription,** receta

**pressure,** presión

**prevent,** prevenir

**prevention,** prevención

**procedure,** procedimiento

**proctologist,** proctólogo

**progesterone,** progesterona

**prognosis,** pronóstico

**prostate gland,** próstata

**protein,** proteína

**psoriasis,** psoriasis

**psychiatrist,** psiquiatra

**psychologist,** psicólogo

**psychosis,** psicosis

**psychotherapy,** psicoterapia

**psychotic,** psicótico

**puberty,** pubertad

**pubic hair,** vello púbico

**pulmonary,** pulmonar

**pulmonary edema,** edema pulmonar

**pulsating,** pulsante

**pulse,** pulso

**pump,** bomba

**pupil,** pupila

**pus,** pus

# Q

**quadriceps,** cuádriceps

**quarantine,** cuarentena

**quinine,** quinina

**quota,** cuota

# R

**rabies,** rabia

**radiation treatment,** tratamiento de radiación

**radiologist,** radiólogo

**radiology,** radiología

**radiotherapy,** radioterapia

**rape,** violación

**rash,** erupción

**reaction,** reacción

**reconstruct,** reconstruir

**recovery,** recuperación

**rectum,** recto

**redness,** enrojecimiento

**refill,** rellenar

**reflex,** reflejo

**reflux,** reflujo

**regurgitation,** regurgitación

**rehabilitate,** rehabilitar

**rehydrate,** rehidratar

**reject,** rechazar

**relapse,** recaída

**relationship (family),** parentesco

**relax,** descansar

**relief,** alivio

**remedy,** remedio

**renal failure,** insuficiencia renal

**replace,** reemplazar

**reproduce,** reproducir

**reproduction,** reproducción

**respirator,** respirador

**respiratory,** respiratorio

**rest,** descansar

**result,** resultado

**resuscitation,** resucitación

**retention,** retención

**retina,** retina

**revive,** reanimarse

**rheumatic fever,** fiebre reumática

**rheumatism,** reumatismo

**rhinoplasty,** rinoplastia

**rhythm method,** método del ritmo

**rib,** costilla

**rigidity,** rigidez

**rigor mortis,** rigor mortis

**risk,** riesgo

**rubella,** rubéola

**runny nose,** secreción nasal

**rupture,** ruptura

# S

**safe,** seguro

**saline,** salino

**saliva,** saliva

**salmonella,** salmonela

**salt,** sal

**sample,** muestra

**sane,** cuerdo

**sanitary,** sanitario

**sanity,** cordura

**sarcoma,** sarcoma

**scab,** costra

**scabies,** sarna

**scald,** escaldadura

**scale,** balanza

**scalp,** cuero cabelludo

**scaly,** escamoso

**scar,** cicatriz

**scarlet fever,** fiebre escarlatina

**schizophrenia,** esquizofrenia

**sciatica,** ciática

**scissors,** tijeras

**scoliosis,** escoliosis

**scratch,** rasguño

**scream,** grito

**screen,** examen de detección

**scrotum,** escroto

**scurvy,** escorbuto

**sealant,** sellador

**seasickness,** mareo (en un barco)

**secrete,** secretar

**secretion,** secreción

**sedative,** sedante

**sedentary,** sedentario

**seizures,** convulsiones

**semen,** semen

**senile,** senil

**senility,** senilidad

**sensation,** sensación

**sensitive,** sensible

**sensitivity,** sensibilidad

**septum,** tabique

**serious,** serio

**serum,** suero

**severe,** severo

**sex,** sexo

**sexuality,** sexualidad

**shakes,** temblores

**sharp (pain),** agudo (dolor)

**shin,** espinilla

**shingles,** herpes zoster

**shiver,** escalofríos

**shiver,** tiritar

**shock,** choque

**shot,** inyección

**shoulder,** hombro

**shoulder blade,** omóplato

**sibling,** hermano/hermana

**sick,** enfermo

**sickness,** enfermedad

**side,** lado

**side effect,** efecto secundario

**sight,** vista

**sinus,** seno paranasal

**sinusitis,** sinusitis

**skeleton,** esqueleto

**skin,** piel

**skinny,** flaco

**skull,** cráneo

**sleep,** dormir

**sleeping pill,** somnífero

**sleepy,** tener sueño

**sling,** cabestrillo

**slip,** resbalar

**slipped disc,** disco desplazado

**sliver,** astilla

**slur,** arrastrar las palabras

**small intestine,** intestino delgado

**smallpox,** viruela

**smell,** oler

**smoke,** fumar

**snakebite,** mordedura de serpiente

**sneeze,** estornudar

**snore,** roncar

**soap,** jabón

**sober,** sobrio

**social worker,** trabajador social

**sodium,** sodio

**sole (of foot),** planta del pie

**sonogram,** ecografía

**sore,** llaga

**spasm,** espasmo

**specialist,** especialista

**specimen,** muestra/espécimen

**speculum,** espéculo

**speech pathologist,** foniatra

**sperm,** esperma

**spermicide,** espermicida

**sphincter,** esfínter

**spider bite,** picadura de araña

**spina bifida,** espina bífida

**spinal column,** columna vertebral

**spinal cord,** médula espinal

**spleen,** bazo

**splint,** férula

**splint,** entablillar

**splinter,** astilla

**sponge,** esponja

**spots,** manchas

**spotted fever,** fiebre maculosa

**sprain,** torcedura

**sprain,** torcerse

**sputum,** esputo

**stab,** puñalada

**stain,** mancha

**starvation,** inanición

**sterile,** estéril

**sterility,** esterilidad

**sterilize,** esterilizar

**sternum,** esternón

**steroid,** esteroide

**stethoscope,** estetoscopio

**stiff,** rígido

**stimulant,** estimulante

**sting,** picadura de insecto

**sting,** picar

**stirrup,** estribo

**stitches,** puntos de suturas

**stoma,** estoma

**stomach,** estómago

**stomach ache/pain,** dolor de estómago

**stool,** excremento

**strangle,** estrangular

**strength,** fuerza

**strep,** estreptococo

**stress,** estrés

**stretch mark,** estría

**stretcher,** camilla

**stroke,** derrame cerebral

**strong,** fuerte

**stuffy nose,** nariz tapada

**stupor,** estupor

**stutter,** tartamudear

**suffocation,** sofocación

**suicide,** suicidio

**sunburn,** quemadura por el sol

**sunstroke,** insolación

**suppository,** supositorio

**surgeon,** cirujano

**surgery,** cirugía

**surrogate mother,** madre portadora

**survive,** sobrevivir

**suture,** sutura

**swab,** hisopo

**swallow,** tragar

**sweat,** sudor

**swelling,** hinchazón

**swollen,** hinchado

**symptom,** síntoma

**syndrome,** síndrome

**synthetic,** sintético

**syphilis,** sífilis

**syringe,** jeringa

**syrup,** jarabe

# T

**table,** mesa

**tablespoonful,** cucharada

**tablet,** tableta

**tailbone,** cóccix

**take,** tomar

**talcum powder,** talco

**tampon,** tampón

**tapeworm,** teniasis

**taste,** sabor

**taste bud,** papila gustativa

**tattoo,** tatuaje

**tear (of muscle/ligament),** desgarro

**tear (of the eye),** lágrima

**teaspoonful,** cucharadita

**technician,** técnico

**temperature,** temperatura

**temple (of the head),** sien

**temporary,** temporal

**tender,** adolorido

**tendinitis,** tendinitis

**tendon,** tendón

**terminal,** terminal

**test,** prueba/examen

**testicles,** testículos

**testosterone,** testosterona

**tetanus,** tétano

**therapist,** terapeuta

**therapy,** terapia

**thermometer,** termómetro

**thick,** espeso (consistency)/grueso (dimension)

**thigh,** muslo

**thirst,** sed

**thirsty (to be),** tener sed

**thorax,** tórax

**throat,** garganta

**throbbing,** pulsante

**thrombosis,** trombosis

**throw up,** vomitar

**thumb,** pulgar

**thyroid gland,** glándula tiroides

**tincture,** tintura

**tingling,** hormigueo

**tinnitus,** zumbido en los oídos

**tissue,** tejido

**tobacco,** tabaco

**toe,** dedo del pie

**toilet,** inodoro

**tolerate,** tolerar

**tongue,** lengua

**tonic,** tónico

**tonsil,** amígdala

**tonsillectomy,** amigdalectomía

**tonsillitis,** amigdalitis

**tooth,** diente

**toothache,** dolor de muelas

**touch,** tocar

**tourniquet,** torniquete

**towel,** toalla

**toxemia,** toxemia

**toxic,** tóxico

**toxin,** toxina

**trace,** rastro

**trachea,** traquea

**traction,** tracción

**tranquilizers,** tranquilizantes

**transfusion,** transfusión

**transmitted,** transmitido

**transplant,** trasplantar

**trauma,** trauma

**traumatic,** traumático

**treat,** tratar

**treatment,** tratamiento

**tremors,** temblores

**triceps,** tríceps

**trouble,** molestia

**tube,** tubo

**tuberculosis,** tuberculosis

**tumor,** tumor

**tweezers,** pinzas

**twin,** gemelo

**twisted,** torcido

**typhoid fever,** fiebre tifoidea

**typhus,** tifus

# U

**ulcer,** úlcera

**ultrasound,** ultrasonido

**umbilical cord,** cordón umbilical

**uncomfortable,** incómodo

**unconscious,** inconsciente

**unhealthy,** insalubre

**unstable,** inestable

**urethra,** uretra

**urgent,** urgente

**urinal,** orinal

**urinalysis,** examen general de orina

**urinary,** urinario

**urinate,** orinar

**urine,** orina

**urine sample,** muestra de orina

**urologist,** urólogo

**urology,** urología

**uterus,** útero

# V

**vaccinate,** vacunar

**vaccine,** vacuna

**vagina,** vagina

**vaginal,** vaginal

**vaginitis,** vaginitis

**valve,** válvula

**varicose vein,** vena varicosa

**vascular,** vascular

**vasectomy,** vasectomía

**vegetative,** vegetativo

**vein,** vena

**venereal disease,** enfermedad venérea

**venom,** veneno

**ventilator,** ventilador

**ventricle,** ventrículo

**vertebrae,** vértebras

**vertigo,** vértigo

**victim,** víctima

**virile,** viril

**virus,** virus

**vision,** vista

**visiting hours,** horario de visita

**vital,** vital

**vital organ,** órgano vital

**vital signs,** signos vitales

**vitamin,** vitamina

**vocal cord,** cuerda vocal

**vomit,** vomitar

# W

**waist,** cintura

**waiting room,** sala de espera

**wake up,** despertar

**walker,** andador

**ward,** sala

**warning,** aviso

**wart,** verruga

**wash (to),** lavar

**water,** agua

**watery eyes,** ojos llorosos

**weak,** débil

**weakness,** debilidad

**wean,** destetar

**weary,** fatigado

**weigh,** pesar

**weight,** peso

**weight change,** cambio de peso

**wet nurse,** nodriza

**wheel chair,** silla de ruedas

**wheeze,** sibilancia

**wheeze,** respirar con sibilancias

**white blood cells,** glóbulos blancos

**whooping cough (pertussis),** tos ferina

**windpipe,** tráquea

**wisdom tooth,** muela del juicio

**womb,** útero

**worms (intestinal),** lombrices

**wound,** herida

**wrist,** muñeca

# X

**x-rays,** radiografías/rayos X

# Y

**yawn,** bostezar

# SPANISH-ENGLISH
# ESPAÑOL-INGLÉS

# A

**abdomen,** abdomen

**abdominal,** abdominal

**aborto,** abortion

**aborto natural,** miscarriage

**abrasión/raspadura,** abrasion

**absceso,** abscess

**abstinencia,** abstinence

**abuso,** abuse

**ácaro,** mite

**accidente,** accident

**acetaminofén,** acetaminophen

**acidez estomacal,** heartburn

**ácido,** acid

**ácido fólico,** folic acid

**acné,** acne

**aconsejar,** advise (to)

**activo,** active

**adicción,** addiction

**adicción a las drogas,** drug addiction

**adicto,** addict

**adolescencia,** adolescence

**adolorido,** tender

**adoptar,** adopt (to)

**adormecimiento,** numbness

**adrenalina,** adrenaline

**adulto,** adult

**afligirse,** grieve

**agitación,** agitation

**agotamiento,** exhaustion

**agrandamiento,** enlargement

**agua,** water

**agudo,** acute

**agudo (dolor),** sharp (pain)

**aguja,** needle

**ahogamiento,** drowning

**ahogarse,** choke

**aire,** air

**alcoholismo,** alcoholism

**alergia,** allergy

**alérgico,** allergic

**aliento,** breath

**alimentar,** feed

**alimentos,** food

**alivio,** relief

**almohada,** pillow

**altura,** height

**alucinación,** hallucination

**amargo,** bitter

**ambulancia,** ambulance

**amenorrea,** amenorrhea

**amígdala,** tonsil

**amigdalectomía,** tonsillectomy

**amigdalitis,** tonsillitis

**aminoácido,** amino acid

**amnesia,** amnesia

**amniocentesis,** amniocentesis

**amoníaco,** ammonia

**amoratado,** bruised

**ampolla,** blister

**amputar,** amputate (to)

**analgésico,** analgesic

**análisis,** analysis

**anatomía,** anatomy

**anciano,** elderly

**andador,** walker

**anemia,** anemia

**anémico,** anemic

**anestesia,** anesthesia

**anestesiólogo,** anesthesiologist

**aneurisma,** aneurysm/aneurism

**anfetaminas,** amphetamines

**angiograma,** angiogram

**angioplastia,** angioplasty

**angustiado,** distressed

**ano,** anus

**anorexia,** anorexia

**anormal,** abnormal

**anquilostomosis,** hookworm

**ansiedad,** anxiety

**antebrazo,** forearm

**antiácido,** antacid

**antibiótico,** antibiotic

**anticoagulante,** anticoagulant

**anticoncepción,** contraception

**anticuerpos,** antibodies

**antidepresivo,** antidepressant

**antídoto,** antidote

**antihistamínico,** antihistamine

**antojo,** craving

**ántrax,** anthrax

**aorta,** aorta

**aparato ortopédico,** brace

**apatía,** apathy

**apendectomía,** appendectomy

**apendicitis,** appendicitis

**apetito,** appetite

**aplicador,** applicator

**apnea,** apnea

**arrastrar las palabras,** slur

**arritmia,** arrhythmia

**arteria,** artery

**articulación,** joint

**artritis,** arthritis

**asfixia,** asphyxia

**asma,** asthma

**asmático,** asthmatic

**astigmatismo,** astigmatism

**astilla,** sliver

**astilla,** splinter

**ataque cardíaco,** heart attack

**atención a la salud,** health care

**atrofia,** atrophy

**aturdimiento,** daze

**audición,** hearing

**autismo,** autism

**autopsia,** autopsy

**aviso,** warning

**axila,** arm pit

**ayunar,** fast

# B

**babero,** bib

**bacteria,** bacteria

**balanza,** scale

**bañarse,** bathe (to)

**baño,** bath

**barbilla,** chin

**barbitúricos,** barbiturates

**bario,** barium

**bastón,** cane

**bata,** gown

**bazo,** spleen

**bebé,** baby

**bebé,** infant

**benigno,** benign

**bíceps,** biceps

**bicúspide,** bicuspid

**bilirrubina,** bilirubin

**bilis,** bile

**biológico,** biological

**biopsia,** biopsy

**bizco,** cross-eyed

**boca,** mouth

**boca abajo,** face down

**boca arriba,** face up

**bocio,** goiter

**bolsa amniótica,** amniotic sac

**bomba,** pump

**borracho,** drunk

**bostezar,** yawn

**botella,** bottle

**botulismo,** botulism

**brazo,** arm

**bronquitis,** bronchitis

**bulimia,** bulimia

**bulímico,** bulimic

**bulto,** lump

**bursitis,** bursitis

# C

**cabestrillo,** sling

**cabeza,** head

**cadera,** hip

**caída,** fall

**calambre,** cramp

**calcificado,** calcified

**calcio,** calcium

**cálculos biliares,** gallstones

**cálculos renales,** kidney stones

**callo,** callus

**callo,** corn (callus)

**calmante para el dolor,** pain reliever

**caloría,** calorie

**calvicie,** baldness

**calvo,** bald

**cama,** bed

**cambio de peso,** weight change

**camilla,** gurney

**camilla,** stretcher

**cáncer,** cancer

**canceroso,** cancerous

**capilar,** capillary

**cápsula,** capsule

**cara,** face

**carbohidrato,** carbohydrate

**carcinogénico,** carcinogenic

**carcinoma,** carcinoma

**cardíaco,** cardiac

**cardiología,** cardiology

**cardiólogo,** cardiologist

**cartílago,** cartilage

**caspa,** dandruff

**castración,** castration

**catarata,** cataract

**catatónico,** catatonic

**catéter,** catheter

**cateterismo,** catheterization

**cateterizar,** catheterize

**causa,** cause

**cauterizar,** cauterize

**ceceo,** lisp

**ceguera,** blindness

**ceja,** eyebrow

**cerebro,** brain

**choque,** shock

**cicatriz,** scar

**ciclo menstrual,** menstrual cycle

**ciego,** blind

**cigarrillo,** cigarette

**cintura,** waist

**circulación,** circulation

**circuncisión,** circumcision

**cirrosis,** cirrhosis

**cirugía,** surgery

**cirujano,** surgeon

**cita,** appointment

**clamidia,** chlamydia

**claustrofobia,** claustrophobia

**clavícula,** collarbone

**clínica,** clinic

**clítoris,** clitoris

**coágulo,** clot

**cocaína,** cocaine

**cóccix,** coccyx

**cóccix,** tailbone

**codeína,** codeine

**codo,** elbow

**cojín eléctrico,** heating pad

**colágeno,** collagen

**cólera,** cholera

**colesterol,** cholesterol

**cólico,** colic

**cólicos menstruales,** cramps (menstrual)

**colitis,** colitis

**colon,** colon

**colonoscopía,** colonoscopy

**colostomia,** colostomy

**columna vertebral,** backbone

**columna vertebral,** spinal column

**coma,** coma

**comatoso,** comatose

**comezón,** itch

**cómodo,** comfortable

**complicación,** complication

**compresa,** compress

**concebir,** conceive

**condón,** condom

**conducta,** behavior

**confundido,** confused

**confusión,** confusion

**congelar,** freeze

**congénito,** congenital

**congestión,** congestion

**conjuntiva,** conjunctiva

**conjuntivitis,** conjunctivitis

**conmoción cerebral,** concussion

**conocimiento,** consciousness

**consciente,** conscious

**consentir,** consent

**consultorio,** doctor's office

**consultorio,** office

**contagioso,** contagious

**contaminado,** contaminated

**contracciones,** contractions

**contusión,** contusion

**convaleciente,** convalescent

**convulsión,** convulsion

**convulsiones,** seizures

**corazón,** heart

**cordón umbilical,** umbilical cord

**cordura,** sanity

**coronario,** coronary

**cortar,** cut

**cortisona,** cortisone

**costilla,** rib

**costra,** scab

**cráneo,** cranium

**cráneo,** skull

**crecimiento,** growth

**crítico,** critical

**crónico,** chronic

**crup,** croup

**cuádriceps,** quadriceps

**cuarentena,** quarantine

**cucharada,** tablespoonful

**cucharadita,** teaspoonful

**cuchillo,** knife

**cuello,** neck

**cuello del útero,** cervix

**cuerda vocal,** vocal cord

**cuerdo,** sane

**cuero cabelludo,** scalp

**cuerpo,** body

**cuidado,** care

**cuidado prenatal,** prenatal care

**culpa,** guilt

**cultivo,** culture

**cuna,** crib

**cuota,** quota

**curandero,** folk healer

**curar,** cure

**curarse,** heal

**curita,** bandaid

**cutícula,** cuticle

# CH

**chupete,** pacifier

**ciática,** sciatica

# D

**daltonismo,** color-blindness

**dañado,** impaired

**dañar,** harm

**dañino,** harmful

**dar de alta,** discharge from hospital

**débil,** weak

**debilidad,** weakness

**dedo (de la mano),** finger

**dedo del pie,** toe

**defecar,** defecate

**deficiencia,** deficiency

**deformado,** deformed

**deformidad,** deformity

**delirante,** delirious

**delirio,** delirium

**deltoides,** deltoids

**demencia,** dementia

**dentadura postiza,** denture

**dental,** dental

**dentista,** dentist

**depresión,** depression

**dermatitis,** dermatitis

**dermatólogo,** dermatologist

**derrame cerebral,** stroke

**desarrollar,** develop

**descansar,** relax

**descansar,** rest

**descongestionante,** decongestant

**deseo sexual,** libido

**desfibrilación,** defibrillation

**desfibrilador,** defibrillator

**desgarro,** tear (of muscle/ligament)

**deshidratación,** dehydration

**desinfectante,** disinfectant

**desinfectar,** disinfect

**desintoxicación,** detoxification

**desmayarse,** faint

**desmayos,** fainting spells

**desnudo,** naked

**desnutrición,** malnutrition

**desorientación,** disorientation

**despertar,** awaken (to)

**despertar,** wake up

**despierto,** awake

**despigmentación,** depigmentation

**después de la operación,** post-op

**destetar,** wean

**deterioro,** deterioration

**diabetes,** diabetes

**diafragma,** diaphragm

**diagnosticar,** diagnose

**diagnóstico,** diagnosis

**diálisis,** dialysis

**diariamente,** daily

**diarrea,** diarrhea

**diente,** tooth

**diente impactado,** impacted tooth

**dientes postizos,** false teeth

**dieta,** diet

**dietista,** dietitian

**difteria,** diphtheria

**difunto,** deceased

**digerir,** digest

**digestión,** digestion

**dilatación,** dilation

**dilatado,** dilated

**diluir,** dilute

**discapacidad,** disability

**disco desplazado,** disk (slipped)

**disco desplazado,** slipped disc

**disentería,** dysentery

**dislexia,** dyslexia

**dislocación,** dislocation

**distender,** distend

**distrofia,** dystrophy

**diurético,** diuretic

**doler,** hurt

**dolor,** ache

**dolor,** pain

**dolor de cabeza,** headache

**dolor de estómago,** stomach ache/pain

**dolor de muelas,** toothache

**dolor de oído,** earache

**dolores de parto,** labor pains

**doloroso,** painful

**donante,** donor

**dormir,** sleep

**dosis,** dosage

**drogas,** drugs (usually illicit)

**duodeno,** duodenum

# E

**eccema,** eczema

**ecografía,** sonogram

**edema,** edema

**edema pulmonar,** pulmonary edema

**efecto secundario,** side effect

**ejercicio,** exercise

**electrocardiograma,** EKG

**electrocardiograma,** electrocardiogram

**electrocución,** electrocution

**elixir,** elixir

**embarazada,** pregnant

**embarazo,** pregnancy

**embolia,** embolism

**embrión,** embryo

**emergencia,** emergency

**empaste,** filling (dental)

**enanismo,** dwarfism

**encamado,** bedridden (patient)

**encefalitis,** encephalitis

**encías,** gums

**endémico,** endemic

**endocrino,** endocrine

**endocrinólogo,** endocrinologist

**endorfina,** endorphin

**endoscopía,** endoscopy

**endurecimiento,** hardening

**enema,** enema

**enfermedad,** ailment

**enfermedad,** disease

**enfermedad,** illness

**enfermedad,** sickness

**enfermedad de Crohn,** Crohn's disease

**enfermedad venérea,** venereal disease

**enfermera,** nurse

**enfermo,** ill

**enfermo,** sick

**enfisema pulmonar,** pulmonary emphysema

**enojo,** anger

**enrojecimiento,** redness

**entablillar,** splint

**enuresis,** bed-wetting

**enzima,** enzyme

**epidémico/epidemia,** epidemic

**epidural,** epidural

**epiglotis,** epiglottis

**epilepsia,** epilepsy

**equilibrio,** balance

**erección,** erection

**eructar,** burp

**eructo,** belch

**erupción,** rash

**escaldadura,** scald

**escalofríos,** chills

**escalofríos,** shiver

**escama,** flake

**escamoso,** scaly

**escoliosis,** scoliosis

**escorbuto,** scurvy

**escroto,** scrotum

**escuálido,** emaciated

**escuchar,** listen

**esfínter,** sphincter

**esfuerzo,** exertion

**esófago,** esophagus

**espalda,** back

**espasmo,** spasm

**especialista,** specialist

**espéculo,** speculum

**esperma,** sperm

**espermicida,** spermicide

**espeso (consistency)/grueso (dimension),** thick

**espina bífida,** spina bifida

**espinilla,** shin

**espinillas,** blackheads

**espinillas,** pimples

**esponja,** sponge

**espuma,** foam

**esputo,** sputum

**esqueleto,** skeleton

**esquizofrenia,** schizophrenia

**estar congestionado,** congested (to be)

**estéril,** infertile

**estéril,** sterile

**esterilidad,** sterility

**esterilizar,** sterilize

**esternón,** breastbone

**esternón,** sternum

**esteroide,** steroid

**estetoscopio,** stethoscope

**estilo de vida,** lifestyle

**estimulante,** stimulant

**estoma,** stoma

**estómago,** stomach

**estornudar,** sneeze

**estrangular,** strangle

**estreñimiento,** constipation

**estreptococo,** strep

**estrés,** stress

**estría,** stretch mark

**estribo,** stirrup

**estrógeno,** estrogen

**estupor,** stupor

**éter,** ether

**euforia,** euphoria

**eutanasia,** euthanasia

**examen,** checkup

**examen,** exam

**examen de detección,** screen

**examen de Papanicolaou,** Pap smear

**examen de seguimiento,** follow-up

**examen general de orina,** urinalysis

**examinar,** examine

**excremento,** excrement

**excremento,** stool

**exfoliación,** exfoliation

**exhalar,** exhale

**expectorante,** expectorant

**expediente médico,** medical record

**experto,** expert

**explicar,** explain

**exposición,** exposure

**externo,** external

**extracción,** extraction

**extraer,** extract

**extremidad,** limb

**extremidad lisiada,** lame extremity

**eyacular,** ejaculate

# F

**faringe,** pharynx

**farmacéutico,** pharmacist

**farmacia,** pharmacy

**fatal/mortal,** fatal

**fatiga,** fatigue

**fatigado,** weary

**fecha aproximada de parto,** due date

**fecundación,** impregnation

**fémur,** femur

**fértil,** fertile

**fertilización,** fertilization

**férula,** splint

**feto,** fetus

**fibra,** fiber

**fibrilación,** fibrillation

**fibrosis quística,** cystic fibrosis

**fiebre,** fever

**fiebre escarlatina,** scarlet fever

**fiebre maculosa,** spotted fever

**fiebre reumática,** rheumatic fever

**fiebre tifoidea,** typhoid fever

**fisioterapia,** physical therapy

**fisura,** fissure

**flaco,** skinny

**flatulencia,** flatulence

**flema,** phlegm

**flexible,** flexible

**fluoruro,** fluoride

**fobia,** phobia

**folículo,** follicle

**foniatra,** speech pathologist

**fórceps,** forceps

**fórmula,** formula

**formulario,** form

**fosa nasal,** nostril

**fósforo,** phosphorus

**fotosensibilidad,** photosensitivity

**fractura,** fracture

**frecuencia,** frequency

**frenos dentales,** braces (dental)

**frente,** forehead

**frío/a,** cold

**fuego/incendio,** fire

**fuerte,** strong

**fuerza,** strength

**fumar,** smoke

**función,** function

# G

**gafas,** glasses

**ganglios linfáticos,** lymph nodes

**gangrena,** gangrene

**garganta,** throat

**gas,** gas

**gas hilarante (óxido nitroso),** laughing gas

**gasa,** gauze

**gastritis,** gastritis

**gastroenterólogo,** gastroenterologist

**gastrointestinal,** gastrointestinal (GI)

**gatear,** crawl

**gel,** gel

**gemelo,** twin

**genes,** genes

**genético,** genetic

**genitales,** genitals

**geriátrico,** geriatric

**germen,** germ

**gestación,** gestation

**giardia,** giardia

**gigantismo,** gigantism

**ginecología,** gynecology

**ginecólogo,** gynecologist

**gingivitis,** gingivitis

**glándula,** gland

**glándula tiroides,** thyroid gland

**glaucoma,** glaucoma

**glóbulos blancos,** white blood cells

**glucosa,** glucose

**gluten,** gluten

**glúteo,** buttock

**gonorrea,** gonorrhea

**gordo,** fat (person)

**gota,** gout

**gotas,** drops

**gotero,** dropper

**gramo,** gram

**grasa,** fat (food)

**gripe,** flu

**gripe,** influenza

**grito,** scream

**guante,** glove

# H

**hábito,** habit

**hacer gárgaras,** gargle

**heces,** feces

**helicóptero,** helicopter

**hematoma,** hematoma

**hemofilia,** hemophilia

**hemoglobina,** hemoglobin

**hemorragia,** hemorrhage

**hepatitis,** hepatitis

**hereditario,** hereditary

**herencia,** heredity

**herida,** wound

**hermafrodita,** hermaphrodite

**hermano/hermana,** sibling

**hernia,** hernia

**heroína,** heroin

**herpes,** herpes

**herpes labial,** cold sores

**herpes zoster,** shingles

**heterosexual,** heterosexual

**hidratar,** hydrate

**hierba,** herb

**hierro,** iron

**hígado,** liver

**higiene,** hygiene

**himen,** hymen

**hinchado,** swollen

**hinchazón,** swelling

**hiperactivo,** hyperactive

**hiperglucemia,** hyperglycemia

**hipersensibilidad,** hypersensitivity

**hipertermia,** hyperthermia

**hipertiroidismo,** hyperthyroidism

**hiperventilación,** hyperventilation

**hipo,** hiccups

**hipocondria,** hypochondria

**hipoglucemia,** hypoglycemia

**hipotálamo,** hypothalamus

**hipotermia,** hypothermia

**hipotiroidismo,** hypothyroidism

**hipoxia,** hypoxia

**hisopo,** swab

**histerectomía,** hysterectomy

**histeria,** hysteria

**hombro,** shoulder

**homeopatía,** homeopathy

**homosexual,** homosexual

**hongo,** fungus

**horario de visita,** visiting hours

**hormigueo,** tingling

**hormona,** hormone

**hormonal,** hormonal

**hospital,** hospital

**hueso,** bone

**huevo/óvulo,** egg

# I

**ibuprofeno,** ibuprofen

**ictericia/piel amarilla,** jaundice

**implantar,** implant

**impotencia,** impotence

**inanición,** starvation

**incapacidad,** impairment

**incesto,** incest

**incisión,** incision

**incómodo,** uncomfortable

**inconsciente,** unconscious

**incontinencia,** incontinence

**incubadora,** incubator

**incurable,** incurable

**indigestión,** indigestion

**inducir,** induce

**inestable,** unstable

**infancia,** childhood

**infección,** infection

**infectar,** infect

**infertilidad,** infertility

**inflamación,** inflammation

**ingerir,** ingest

**ingle,** groin

**ingresar,** admit (into hospital)

**inhalador,** inhaler

**inhalar,** inhale

**injerto,** graft

**inmaduro,** immature

**inmóvil,** immobile

**inmovilización,** immobilization

**inmune,** immune

**inmunizar,** immunize

**inoculación,** inoculation

**inocular,** inoculate

**inodoro,** toilet

**inofensivo,** harmless

**insalubre,** unhealthy

**inseminación,** insemination

**insolación,** heat-stroke

**insolación,** sunstroke

**insomnio,** insomnia

**instrumento,** instrument

**insuficiencia renal,** kidney failure

**insuficiencia renal,** renal failure

**insulina,** insulin

**internar,** hospitalize

**internista,** internist

**interno,** internal

**intestino,** bowel

**intestino,** intestine

**intestino delgado,** small intestine

**intestino grueso,** large intestine

**intestino/tripas,** gut

**intoxicación,** intoxication

**intubación,** intubation

**inyección,** shot

**inyectar,** inject

**irrigar,** irrigate

**irritación,** irritation

# J

**jabón,** soap

**jalea,** jelly

**jarabe,** syrup

**jeringa,** syringe

**jorobado,** hunchback

**juanete,** bunion

**jugo,** juice

# L

**laberintitis,** labyrinthitis

**labios,** lips

**laboratorio,** laboratory

**laceración,** laceration

**lactancia,** lactation

**lactosa,** lactose

**ladillas,** crabs

**lado,** side

**lágrima,** tear (of the eye)

**laparoscopía,** laparoscopy

**laringe,** larynx

**laringitis,** laryngitis

**látex,** latex

**latido del corazón,** heartbeat

**latidos cardíacos irregulares,** irregular heartbeat

**lavar,** wash (to)

**laxante,** laxative

**lengua,** tongue

**lenguaje,** language

**lepra,** leprosy

**lesbiana,** lesbian

**lesión,** injury

**lesión,** lesion

**letargo,** lethargy

**leucemia,** leukemia

**libra,** pound

**ligamento,** ligament

**linfa,** lymph

**linfoma,** lymphoma

**linimento,** liniment

**liposucción,** liposuction

**líquido,** liquid

**líquidos intravenosos,** intravenous fluids

**lisiado,** crippled

**lisiar,** cripple

**llaga,** sore

**llorar,** cry

**lobotomía,** lobotomy

**lóbulo,** earlobe

**lóbulo,** lobe

**loco,** insane

**locura,** insanity

**lombrices,** worms (intestinal)

**lubricar,** lubricate

**lunar,** birthmark

**lunar,** mole

**lupus,** lupus

# M

**madre portadora,** surrogate mother

**madurez,** maturity

**mal aliento,** halitosis

**malabsorción,** malabsorption

**malestar,** malaise

**malformación,** malformation

**maligno,** malignant

**malo(a),** bad

**mamografía,** mammogram

**mancha,** stain

**manchas,** spots

**mandíbula,** jaw

**manía,** mania

**maníaco depresivo,** manic-depressive

**mano,** hand

**marcapaso,** pacemaker

**mareado,** dizzy

**mareo (en un barco),** seasickness

**mareos,** dizziness

**marihuana,** marijuana

**martillo de reflejos,** hammer

**masa,** mass

**masajear,** massage/rub

**máscara,** mask

**mastectomía,** mastectomy

**masticar,** chew

**materno,** maternal

**medicamento,** medication

**medicina,** medicine

**medicinas,** drugs (legal)

**médico,** doctor

**médico,** physician

**médula espinal,** spinal cord

**mejilla,** cheek

**melanoma,** melanoma

**meningitis,** meningitis

**menopausia,** menopause

**menstruación,** menses

**menstruación,** menstruation

**mente,** mind

**mesa,** table

**metabolismo,** metabolism

**metadona,** methadone

**metanfetamina,** methamphetamine

**metástasis,** metastasis

**método del ritmo,** rhythm method

**microcirugía,** microsurgery

**microscopio,** microscope

**miedo,** fear

**migraña,** migraine

**miopía,** myopia

**miopía,** nearsightedness

**moler,** grind

**molestia,** trouble

**monitor,** monitor

**monitor fetal,** fetal monitor

**mononucleosis,** mononucleosis

**mordedura,** bite

**mordedura de serpiente,** snakebite

**moretón,** bruise

**morfina,** morphine

**morgue,** morgue

**morir,** die

**mortalidad,** mortality

**mucoso/mucosa,** mucous

**mudo,** mute

**muela del juicio,** wisdom tooth

**muerte,** death

**muerto,** dead

**muestra,** sample

**muestra de orina,** urine sample

**muestra/espécimen,** specimen

**muletas,** crutches

**muñeca,** wrist

**músculo,** muscle

**músculo posterior del muslo,** hamstring

**muslo,** thigh

**mutación,** mutation

# N

**nacimiento prematuro,** premature birth

**nacimiento/parto,** birth

**narcolepsia,** narcolepsy

**narcótico,** narcotic

**nariz,** nose

**nariz tapada,** stuffy nose

**natural,** natural

**náuseas,** nausea

**negligencia médica,** malpractice

**nervio,** nerve

**nervioso,** nervous

**neuralgia,** neuralgia

**neurología,** neurology

**neurólogo,** neurologist

**neurosis,** neurosis

**neurótico,** neurotic

**nicotina,** nicotine

**nitroglicerina,** nitroglycerine

**nodriza,** wet nurse

**normal,** normal

**nuca,** nape

**nudillo,** knuckle

**nudo,** knot

**nutrición,** nourishment

**nutrición,** nutrition

**nutricionista,** nutritionist

**nutriente,** nutrient

# O

**obesidad,** obesity

**obeso,** obese

**obstetra,** obstetrician

**obstetricia,** obstetrics

**obstrucción,** blockage

**obstrucción,** obstruction

**oclusión,** occlusion

**oftalmólogo,** ophthalmologist

**oído,** ear (inner)

**oído medio,** ear (middle)

**oír,** hear

**ojo,** eye

**ojos llorosos,** watery eyes

**oler,** smell

**olor,** odor

**ombligo,** bellybutton

**ombligo,** navel

**omóplato,** shoulder blade

**oncología,** oncology

**oncólogo,** oncologist

**operar,** operate

**óptico,** optic

**optometrista,** optometrist

**oral,** oral

**oreja,** ear (outer)

**órgano,** organ

**órgano vital,** vital organ

**orgasmo,** orgasm

**orina,** urine

**orinal,** bedpan

**orinal,** urinal

**orinar,** urinate

**ortodoncista,** orthodontist

**ortopedia,** orthopedics

**ortopedista,** orthopedist

**osteoartritis,** osteoarthritis

**osteópata,** osteopath

**osteoporosis,** osteoporosis

**ovario,** ovary

**ovulación,** ovulation

**ovular,** ovulate

**oxígeno,** oxygen

# P

**paciente,** patient

**padrastro,** hangnail

**paladar,** palate

**paladar hendido,** cleft palate

**palangana,** basin

**palidez,** paleness

**pálido,** pale

**palpitaciones,** palpitations

**paludismo,** malaria

**páncreas,** pancreas

**pantorilla,** calf (of leg)

**pañal,** diaper

**paperas,** mumps

**papila gustativa,** taste bud

**parálisis,** paralysis

**paralítico,** paralyzed

**paramédico,** paramedic

**paranoia,** paranoia

**parapléjico,** paraplegic

**parásito,** parasite

**parche,** patch

**parentesco,** relationship (family)

**parpadear,** blink

**párpado,** eyelid

**partera,** midwife

**parto,** childbirth

**parto,** delivery (of a baby)

**pastillas para la garganta,** lozenges

**paterno,** paternal

**patólogo,** pathologist

**peca,** freckle

**pecho,** chest

**pecho/seno,** breast/chest

**pediatra,** pediatrician

**pediatría,** pediatrics

**pediátrico,** pediatric

**peligro,** danger

**pelo,** hair

**pelvis,** pelvis

**pene,** penis

**penetrar,** penetrate

**penicilina,** penicillin

**perforación,** perforation

**peróxido de hidrógeno,** hydrogen peroxide

**pesadilla,** nightmare

**pesar,** grief

**pesar,** weigh

**peso,** weight

**pestaña,** eyelash

**pezón,** nipple

**picadura,** bite (insect)

**picadura de araña,** spider bite

**picadura de insecto,** sting

**picar,** sting

**pie,** foot

**pie de atleta,** athlete's foot

**pie plano,** flat foot

**piel,** skin

**piel de gallina,** goose bumps

**pierna,** leg

**pies,** feet

**píldora,** pill

**pinzas,** tweezers

**piojos,** lice

**pistola,** gun

**placa,** plaque

**placenta,** afterbirth

**placenta,** placenta

**plaga,** plague

**planificación familiar,** family planning

**planta del pie,** sole (of foot)

**plaquetas,** platelets

**plasma,** plasma

**plomo,** lead

**podólogo,** podiatrist

**polen,** pollen

**poliomielitis,** polio

**pólipo,** polyp

**polvo,** dust

**polvo,** powder

**poro,** pore

**posparto,** postpartum

**postmenopáusico,** postmenopausal

**potasio,** potassium

**pre eclampsia,** preeclampsia

**pre menopáusico,** premenopausal

**predisponer,** predispose

**prepucio,** foreskin

**presión,** pressure

**presión alta,** high blood pressure

**presión alta,** hypertension

**presión baja,** low blood pressure

**prevención,** prevention

**prevenir,** prevent

**primeros auxilios,** first aid

**procedimiento,** procedure

**proctólogo,** proctologist

**progesterona,** progesterone

**pronóstico,** prognosis

**próstata,** prostate gland

**proteína,** protein

**protuberancia,** bump

**provocar náuseas,** gag

**prueba/examen,** test

**psicólogo,** psychologist

**psicosis,** psychosis

**psicoterapia,** psychotherapy

**psicótico,** psychotic

**psiquiatra,** psychiatrist

**psoriasis,** psoriasis

**pubertad,** puberty

**pulgar,** thumb

**pulmonar,** pulmonary

**pulmones,** lungs

**pulmonía,** pneumonia

**pulsante,** pulsating

**pulsante,** throbbing

**pulso,** pulse

**puntos de suturas,** stitches

**puñalada,** stab

**puño,** fist

**pupila,** pupil

**pus,** pus

# Q

**quebrar,** break

**queja,** complaint

**quemadura,** burn

**quemadura por el sol,** sunburn

**químico,** chemical

**quimioterapia,** chemotherapy

**quinina,** quinine

**quiropráctico,** chiropractor

**quiste,** cyst

# R

**rabia,** rabies

**radiografías/rayos X,** x-rays

**radiología,** radiology

**radiólogo,** radiologist

**radioterapia,** radiotherapy

**rasguño,** scratch

**rastro,** trace

**reacción,** reaction

**reanimación cardiopulmonar,** CPR

**reanimarse,** revive

**recaída,** relapse

**receta,** prescription

**recetar,** prescribe

**rechazar,** reject

**reconstruir,** reconstruct

**recto,** rectum

**recuperación,** recovery

**reemplazar,** replace

**reflejo,** reflex

**reflujo,** reflux

**regurgitación,** regurgitation

**rehabilitar,** rehabilitate

**rehidratar,** rehydrate

**relaciones sexuales,** intercourse

**rellenar,** refill

**remedio,** remedy

**reproducción,** reproduction

**reproducir,** reproduce

**resaca,** hangover

**resbalar,** slip

**resfriado común,** cold (illness)

**respirador,** respirator

**respirar,** breathe

**respirar con sibilancias,** wheeze

**respiratorio,** respiratory

**resucitación,** resuscitation

**resultado,** result

**retención,** retention

**retina,** retina

**reumatismo,** rheumatism

**riesgo,** risk

**rigidez,** rigidity

**rígido,** stiff

**rigor mortis,** rigor mortis

**rinoplastia,** rhinoplasty

**riñón,** kidney

**rodilla,** knee

**roncar,** snore

**ronchas,** hives

**ronco,** hoarse

**ronquera,** hoarseness

**roto,** broken

**rótula,** kneecap

**rozar,** chafe

**rubéola,** German measles

**rubéola,** rubella

**rubor,** flush

**ruptura,** rupture

# S

**sabor,** taste

**sacar sangre,** draw blood

**sal,** salt

**sala,** ward

**sala de espera,** waiting room

**salino,** saline

**saliva,** saliva

**salmonela,** salmonella

**salud,** health

**sangrar,** bleed

**sangre,** blood

**sanguijuela,** leech

**sanitario,** sanitary

**sano,** healthy

**sarampión,** measles

**sarcoma,** sarcoma

**sarna,** scabies

**secreción,** discharge

**secreción,** secretion

**secreción nasal,** runny nose

**secretar,** secrete

**sed,** thirst

**sedante,** sedative

**sedentario,** sedentary

**seguro,** insurance

**seguro,** safe

**sellador,** sealant

**semen,** semen

**senil,** senile

**senilidad,** senility

**seno paranasal,** sinus

**sensación,** sensation

**sensibilidad,** sensitivity

**sensible,** sensitive

**sentir,** feel

**sequedad,** dryness

**serio,** serious

**severo,** severe

**sexo,** gender

**sexo,** sex

**sexualidad,** sexuality

**shock anafiláctico,** anaphylactic

**sibilancia,** wheeze

**sien,** temple (of the head)

**siesta,** nap

**sífilis,** syphilis

**signos vitales,** vital signs

**silla de ruedas,** wheel chair

**síndrome,** syndrome

**sintético,** synthetic

**síntoma,** symptom

**sinusitis,** sinusitis

**sobredosis,** overdose

**sobrepeso,** overweight

**sobrevivir,** survive

**sobrio,** sober

**sodio,** sodium

**sofocación,** suffocation

**sofocos,** hot flashes

**somnífero,** sleeping pill

**somnoliento,** drowsy

**sordera,** deafness

**sordo,** deaf

**sordo (dolor),** dull (pain)

**sordomudo,** deaf-mute

**subir de peso,** gain weight

**sudor,** sweat

**suero,** serum

**suicidio,** suicide

**supositorio,** suppository

**supurar,** drain

**suspender,** discontinue

**susto,** fright

**sutura,** suture

# T

**tabaco,** tobacco

**tabique,** septum

**tableta,** tablet

**tajo,** gash

**talco,** talcum powder

**talón,** heel

**tampón,** tampon

**tapones para los oídos,** earplugs

**tartamudear,** stutter

**tatuaje,** tattoo

**técnico,** technician

**tejido,** tissue

**temblores,** shakes

**temblores,** tremors

**temperatura,** temperature

**temporal,** temporary

**tendinitis,** tendinitis

**tendón,** tendon

**tener sed,** thirsty (to be)

**tener sueño,** sleepy

**teniasis,** tapeworm

**terapeuta,** therapist

**terapia,** therapy

**terapia intensiva,** intensive care

**terminal,** terminal

**termómetro,** thermometer

**testículos,** testicles

**testosterona,** testosterone

**tétano,** tetanus

**tétanos,** lockjaw

**tez,** complexion

**tifus,** typhus

**tijeras,** scissors

**tímpano,** eardrum

**tintura,** tincture

**tiña crural,** jock itch

**tiritar,** shiver

**toalla,** towel

**tocar,** touch

**tolerar,** tolerate

**tomar,** take

**tomografía por computadora,** CT scan

**tónico,** tonic

**tórax,** thorax

**torcedura,** sprain

**torcerse,** sprain

**torcido,** twisted

**torniquete,** tourniquet

**tos,** cough

**tos ferina,** pertussis

**tos ferina,** whooping cough (pertussis)

**toser,** cough

**toxemia,** toxemia

**tóxico,** toxic

**toxina,** toxin

**trabajador social,** social worker

**trabajo de parto,** labor

**tracción,** traction

**tragar,** swallow

**tranquilizantes,** tranquilizers

**transfusión,** transfusion

**transmitido,** transmitted

**transpirar,** perspire

**traquea,** trachea

**tráquea,** windpipe

**trasplantar,** transplant

**trastorno,** disorder

**trastorno mental,** mental illness

**tratamiento,** treatment

**tratamiento con láser,** laser treatment

**tratamiento de radiación,** radiation treatment

**tratar,** treat

**trauma,** trauma

**traumático,** traumatic

**tríceps,** triceps

**trombosis,** thrombosis

**trompa de Eustaquio,** Eustachian tube

**trompas de Falopio,** Fallopian tubes

**tuberculosis,** tuberculosis

**tubo,** tube

**tumor,** tumor

**tumorectomía,** lumpectomy

# U

**úlcera,** ulcer

**úlcera gástrica,** gastric ulcer

**ultrasonido,** ultrasound

**ungüento,** ointment

**uña,** nail

**uretra,** urethra

**urgente,** urgent

**urinario,** urinary

**urología,** urology

**urólogo,** urologist

**útero,** uterus

**útero,** womb

# V

**vacuna,** vaccine

**vacuna de refuerzo,** booster shot

**vacunar,** vaccinate

**vagina,** vagina

**vaginal,** vaginal

**vaginitis,** vaginitis

**vahído,** light-headedness

**válvula,** valve

**varicela,** chicken pox

**varón/masculino,** male

**vascular,** vascular

**vasectomía,** vasectomy

**vegetativo,** vegetative

**vejiga,** bladder

**vello,** hair (body)

**vello púbico,** pubic hair

**vena,** vein

**vena varicosa,** varicose vein

**vendaje,** bandage

**veneno,** poison

**veneno,** venom

**ventilador,** ventilator

**ventrículo,** ventricle

**verruga,** wart

**vértebras,** vertebrae

**vértigo,** vertigo

**vesícula biliar,** gall bladder

**víctima,** victim

**vida,** life

**vientre,** belly

**violación,** rape

**viril,** virile

**viruela,** smallpox

**virus,** virus

**vista,** eyesight

**vista,** sight

**vista,** vision

**vista doble,** double vision

**vital,** vital

**vitamina,** vitamin

**vivir,** live

**vivo,** alive

**vomitar,** throw up

**vomitar,** vomit

# Y

**yema,** finger pad

**yerbero,** herbalist

**yeso,** cast

**yodo,** iodine

**yugular,** jugular

# Z

**zumbido,** buzzing

**zumbido en los oídos,** tinnitus

**zurdo,** left-handed

# ABOUT THE AUTHOR

For more than 25 years, José Luis Leyva has worked as a translator and interpreter in various technical areas, including medical environments. His vast experience in bilingualism has allowed him to interpret for directors of medical institutions, prosecutors, forensic experts, specialists and health professionals. He is also the author of other books, including technical dictionaries of the ***Simply, The Key Terms to Learn*** series.

www.ingramcontent.com/pod-product-compliance
Lightning Source LLC
Chambersburg PA
CBHW071358280526
45787CB00001B/370